THE GREAT WALL THROUGH TIME

A 2,700-YEAR JOURNEY ALONG THE WORLD'S GREATEST WALL

ILLUSTRATED BY **DU FEI**

DK | Penguin Random House

LONDON
Project Editor Edward Aves
Editor Sophie Adam
US Editor Megan Douglass
Senior Art Editor Jane Ewart
Designer Annabel Schick
Managing Editors Christine Stroyan, Carine Tracanelli
Managing Art Editor Anna Hall
Production Editor Andy Hilliard
Production Controller Samantha Cross
Jacket Design Development Manager Sophia MTT
Publisher Andrew Macintyre
Associate Publishing Director Liz Wheeler
Art Director Karen Self
Publishing Director Jonathan Metcalf

Consultant William Lindesay
Translator Wu Qi

DELHI
Senior Jacket Designer Suhita Dharamjit
Senior DTP Designer Harish Aggarwal
Senior Jackets Editorial Coordinator Priyanka Sharma

First American Edition, 2022
Published in the United States by DK Publishing
1450 Broadway, Suite 801, New York, NY 10018

Based on an original manuscript by
Encyclopedia of China Publishing House
Retold by Edward Aves

Copyright © 2022 Dorling Kindersley Limited
DK, a Division of Penguin Random House LLC
22 23 24 25 26 10 9 8 7 6 5 4 3 2 1
001–324351–Mar/2022

Artwork copyright © Encyclopedia of China Publishing House, 2022

The publisher would like to thank the following for their kind permission to reproduce their photographs: page 3 Alamy Stock Photo: titoOnz (br)

A catalog record for this book
is available from the Library of Congress.
ISBN: 978-0-7440-4848-3

Printed and bound in China

For the curious
www.dk.com

MIX
Paper from responsible sources
FSC™ C018179

This book was made with Forest Stewardship Council ™ certified paper – one small step in DK's commitment to a sustainable future. For more information go to www.dk.com/our-green-pledge

CONTENTS

Hong Yu the fox

This is Hong Yu, the red fox. Like most foxes, she is clever and cunning—and always hungry. But Hong Yu also has a secret: she can travel through time! Hong Yu is hidden in every picture of the book. Look for her as you travel along the Great Wall, and turn to page 39 for a quiz about her adventures.

The Story of the Great Wall

The Great Wall of China is one of the most incredible building feats in history. It stretches for 13,170 miles (21,196 km), snaking across barren deserts and rugged mountains.

In fact, the Great Wall isn't really one wall at all. It's a whole series of walls, built at different times by different dynasties (ruling families) over thousands of years.

So who built the wall (or walls), and why? For centuries, China's biggest threat came from the north, where nomadic tribesmen often swept down on horseback to raid Chinese villages and farms.

China's first emperor ordered the first Great Wall in 214 BCE to keep out these enemy horsemen. Later emperors built new walls as China's borders shifted this way and that. In time, the Great Wall developed other uses, too. Armies could be transported along it and, as trade developed, it was used to tax goods brought in and out along the Silk Road.

Eventually, the wall was no longer useful and it fell into disrepair. But many sections still survive today. Together, they make up the longest structure ever built.

Join us as we explore this amazing ancient wonder. Our story will transport you through almost 2,700 years of history, stopping off to take in some of the key events in China's past. You'll witness epic battles and meet many colorful characters, from emperors and generals to the everyday folk who built and worked along the wall. Turn the page, and begin an exciting trip through time!

Map of the Great Wall

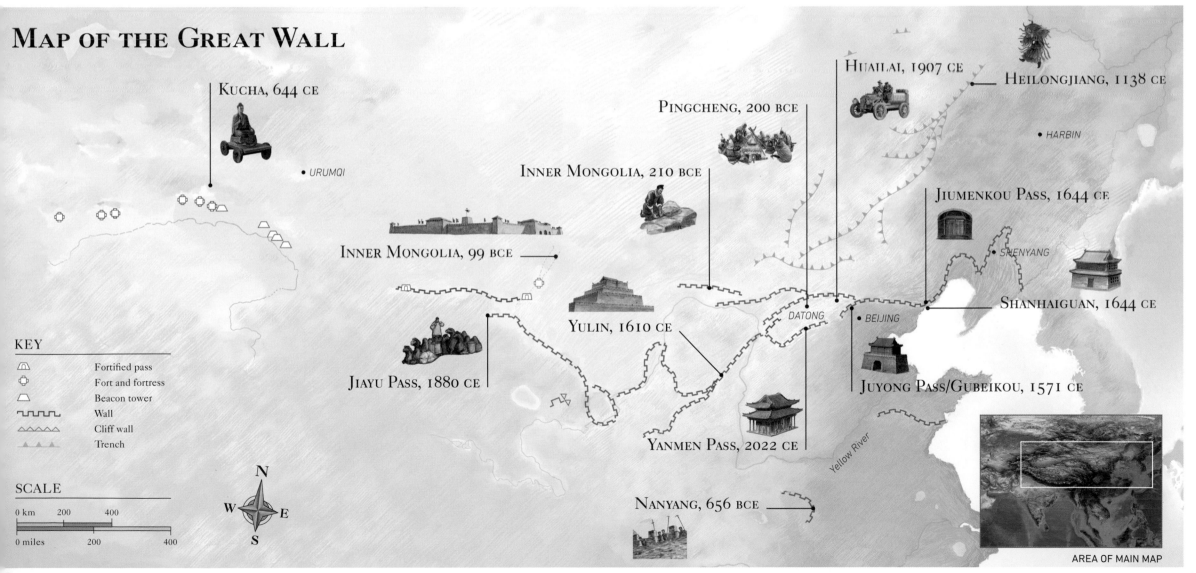

KUCHA, 644 CE

• URUMQI

HUAILAI, 1907 CE

HEILONGJIANG, 1138 CE

PINGCHENG, 200 BCE

• HARBIN

INNER MONGOLIA, 210 BCE

JIUMENKOU PASS, 1644 CE

INNER MONGOLIA, 99 BCE

• SHENYANG

YULIN, 1610 CE

DATONG

• BEIJING

SHANHAIGUAN, 1644 CE

JIAYU PASS, 1880 CE

JUYONG PASS/GUBEIKOU, 1571 CE

YANMEN PASS, 2022 CE

Yellow River

NANYANG, 656 BCE

AREA OF MAIN MAP

KEY

⌂	Fortified pass
✛	Fort and fortress
◠	Beacon tower
⊓⊔⊓⊔	Wall
△△△△	Cliff wall
▲▲▲	Trench

SCALE

0 km   200   400

0 miles   200   400

N W E S

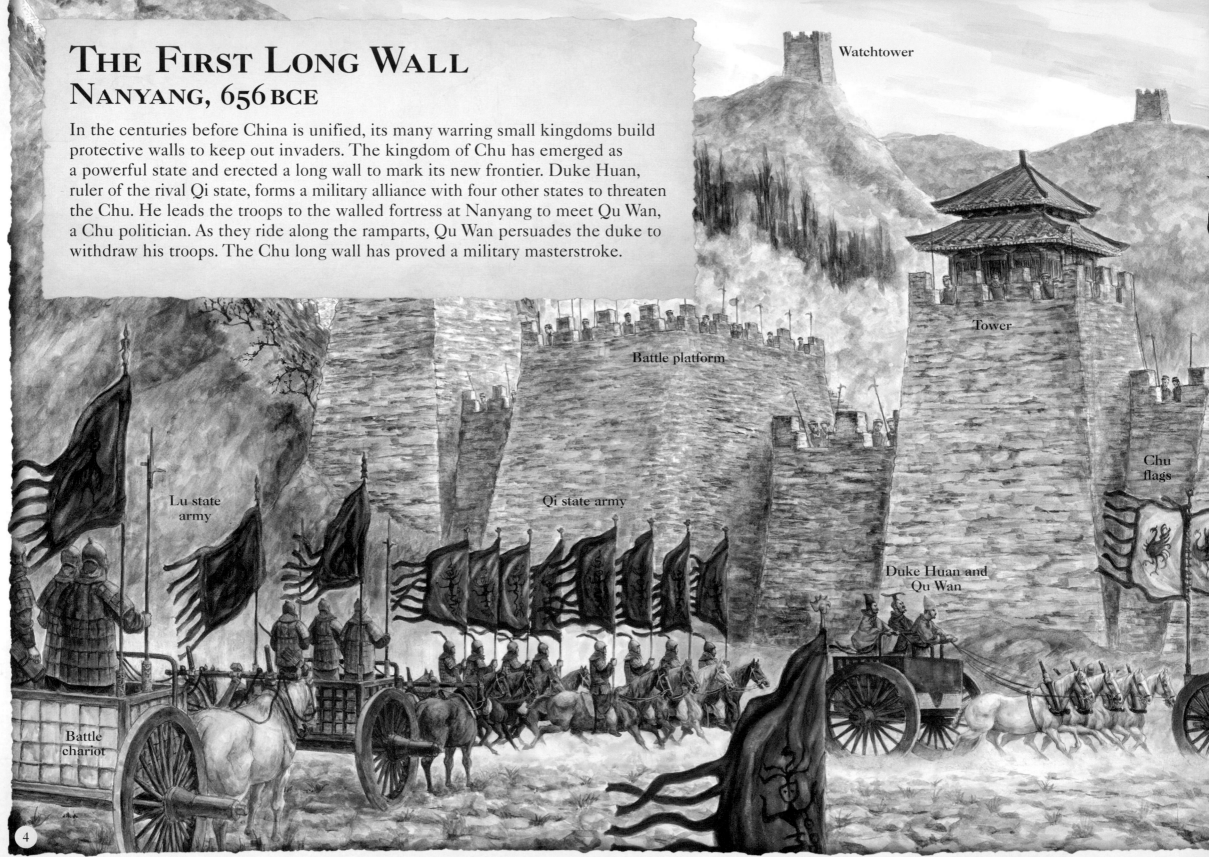

THE FIRST LONG WALL
NANYANG, 656 BCE

In the centuries before China is unified, its many warring small kingdoms build protective walls to keep out invaders. The kingdom of Chu has emerged as a powerful state and erected a long wall to mark its new frontier. Duke Huan, ruler of the rival Qi state, forms a military alliance with four other states to threaten the Chu. He leads the troops to the walled fortress at Nanyang to meet Qu Wan, a Chu politician. As they ride along the ramparts, Qu Wan persuades the duke to withdraw his troops. The Chu long wall has proved a military masterstroke.

Watchtower

Tower

Battle platform

Chu flags

Lu state army

Qi state army

Duke Huan and Qu Wan

Battle chariot

Nobles and important officials ride in chariots pulled by four horses to demonstrate their high-ranking status.

4

Guards can throw heavy boulders down the chute onto attackers.

The five armies in Duke Huan's alliance proudly bear the flags of their state.

These two young guards are nervous on their first day guarding the battlements. Can you find them?

Chu guards

Battlements

Tower

Boulders

Chute

Main gate

Chu chariot

Chen state army

Cao state army

Zheng state army

Zheng soldiers

5

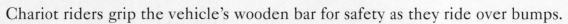

Chariot riders grip the vehicle's wooden bar for safety as they ride over bumps.

Soldiers wear protective tunics made of overlapping pieces of leather.

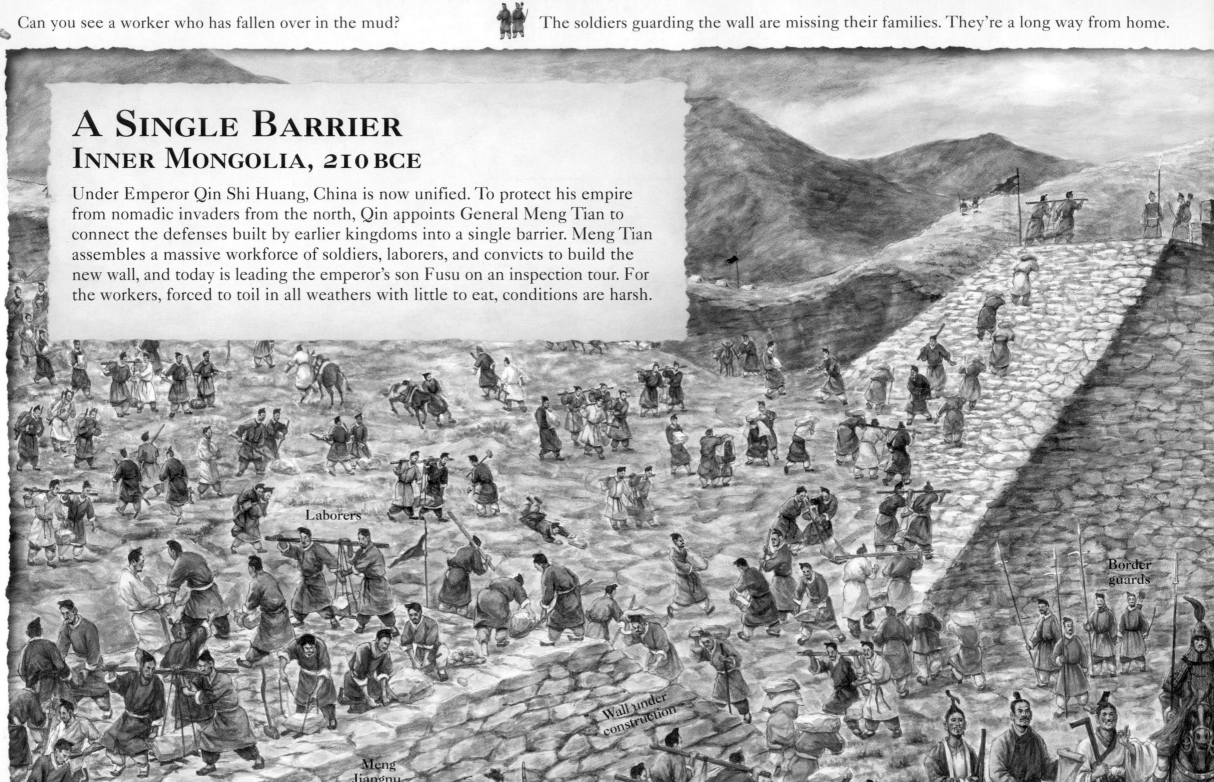

A SINGLE BARRIER
INNER MONGOLIA, 210 BCE

Under Emperor Qin Shi Huang, China is now unified. To protect his empire from nomadic invaders from the north, Qin appoints General Meng Tian to connect the defenses built by earlier kingdoms into a single barrier. Meng Tian assembles a massive workforce of soldiers, laborers, and convicts to build the new wall, and today is leading the emperor's son Fusu on an inspection tour. For the workers, forced to toil in all weathers with little to eat, conditions are harsh.

Laborers

Border guards

Wall under construction

Meng Jiangnu, a widow

Engineers

6

The donkey is complaining at being forced to carry such a heavy load up a steep slope.

The soldiers and workers sleep in tents pitched by the wall.

Yin Mountains

Soldiers' camp

Battlements

Canopy

Meng Tian

Fu

Prince Fusu

Supervisor

Cavalry

Prince Fusu has been put in charge of defending the frontier by the emperor.

A man cooks his dinner in a *fu*, an early type of wok.

The cavalry wear lightweight armor so they can move swiftly if there is an attack.

The emperor's flag is flying high to boost morale—but it isn't working.

A cartload of gifts is being sent to the Xiongnu leader.

Watchtower

Emperor Gaozu's flag

Soldiers' quarters

Han soldiers

Long wall

Emperor Gaozu

Chen Ping

Emperor Gaozu's bodyguard

Xiongnu cavalry

Lou Jing

Emperor Gaozu's chariot

Cart loaded with gifts

Lou Jing, Emperor Gaozu's chief spy at the frontier, warned him of Modun's trap, but the emperor ignored his advice.

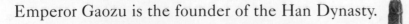

Emperor Gaozu is the founder of the Han Dynasty.

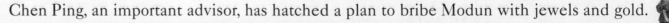

Chen Ping, an important advisor, has hatched a plan to bribe Modun with jewels and gold.

Modun Shanyu is drinking wine in his large *ger* (tent) with his wife.

The Xiongnu cavalry are in high spirits. They are ready to fight.

SIEGE AT MOUNT BAIDENG
PINGCHENG, 200 BCE

The Qin Dynasty has fallen, and following a period of chaos Liu Bang has emerged victorious as China's leader—he is now Emperor Gaozu. But his grip on power is weak. The nomadic tribes on the northern frontier have united as the Xiongnu. Their wily leader, Modun Shanyu, has lured the emperor and his army north of the long wall to frozen Mount Baideng. Here, the Xiongnu cavalry trap the frostbitten Chinese troops in a week-long siege. The emperor's advisors work hard to secure their release, and the two sides eventually agree to respect the wall as the barrier between them.

Modun Shanyu

Xiongnu cavalry

Han soldiers

Fearful of what the future holds, one soldier writes a letter home to his wife and children to tell them he loves them.

9

Wrestling is good training for hand-to-hand combat.

The high jump helps improve strength and agility.

Frame for hoisting lanterns and flags

Juyan Fortress

Fortress guards

Competition judge

Horse racing

Tijianzi (shuttlecock kicking)

Wrestling

High jump

Long jump

Firewood

Firelighting tools

Beacon tower

Horseback archery

Shrine

Material for burning

Army musicians

Guard on duty

Sleeping quarters for soldiers

In *tijianzi*, players keep the shuttlecock in the air using any part of the body except their hands.

Can you spot a rider barely clinging on to the reins?

Troops rake a strip of fine sand so they can detect enemy footprints at night.

A soldier proves his strength by lifting his regiment's cooking cauldron.

MILITARY GAMES
INNER MONGOLIA, 99 BCE

At the Juyan border fortress all eyes are on the annual military games. Beneath the high beacon tower, two teams are locked in a tug of war. Elsewhere, there's polo, archery, martial arts, and horse racing. The games are fun, but they're also valuable military training for the soldiers of Emperor Wudi. Under his rule, the Han Dynasty has expanded China's territory and rebuilt Meng Tian's old walls, which now extend all the way west to the Gobi Desert.

Raked sand

Polo

Archery contest

Pole climbing

Weight training

Cavalry practice

Tug of war

Longbow

Chuiwan (ancient golf)

Cuju (ancient soccer)

Wooden spikes

Archery practice

Crossbow training

One group of soldiers is playing *cuju*, an athletic ball-kicking sport that is similar to modern soccer.

11

Sharp spikes are laid to prevent invaders climbing the tower.

Archers must master the crossbow, a lethal weapon against Xiongnu raids.

Dancers form a circle around a pile of empty water pitchers to pray for rain.

 Monks heave the big Buddha statue into place for the presentation.

The walled fortress of Kucha is one of many defenses built to protect the Silk Road.

RETURN OF A HERO
KUCHA, 644 CE

It's the height of summer and, for the small Buddhist kingdom of Kucha (in modern-day Xinjiang), a day of wild celebration. After many years away, the famous monk Xuanzang is passing through on his way back to China, and is greeted with a hero's welcome. The rulers of the Tang Dynasty, under which China is enjoying a golden age of peace and prosperity, have chosen today to present the people of Kucha with a gift—a giant Buddha statue—to show their friendship. As the festivities unfold, the locals splash water over one another to cool themselves down.

Tian Shan Mountains

Watchtower

Crop fields

Pilgrims

Moat

Walled fortress

Rain dance

Buddha statue

Parasol

Xuanzang

Dancing troupe

Servant

Drummer

Monks

King Kucha

12

 The drummer beats out the dance's rhythm on her double-ended drum.

 Xuanzang is returning home after 15 years studying Buddhism in India.

Sun shelter

Queen of Kucha

Musicians

Observation tower

Ladies-in-waiting

Battlements

Buddhist temples

Gate to the walled fortress

Noblemen

Dancing troupe

Musicians

Kucha guard

Leaping dancers

Servants

Courtiers

Drawbridge

Splash! Can you spot these two strangers hurling water over each other? It's the best way to keep cool.

13

As well as supervising the building work, Wanyan Zongbi is training the soldiers for frontier duty.

Can you spot the soldiers' children flying kites

THE BARRIER IN THE GRASSLANDS
HEILONGJIANG, 1138 CE

In the remote northeastern grasslands, the Jurchen people of the Jin Dynasty dig trenches and build a wall to fend off Mongol attacks. Right now, however, the thud-thud-thud of the workers' tools is accompanied by a stranger sound. Beside the wall, a group of shamans—priests or healers who the Jurchen believe can speak to the spirit world—are performing a ritual dance. As the air fills with their drum beats and cries, the spectacle draws a crowd. But Wanyan Zongbi, the military commander in charge of construction, doesn't mind. He believes the shamans will give his soldiers supernatural powers and inspire the workers to build faster.

Soldiers' tents

Outer trench

Cavalry training

Wanyan Zongbi

Inner trench

Jin Great Wall

Totem pole

Field kitchen

Chef

Dung pile

Messenger

Cart

Shamans dancing

Laborer

In the field kitchen, the chef stands on top of the huge earthenware oven to mix the ingredients in the wok.

14

The shamans dance around the totem pole. They wear colorful costumes with copper mirrors and bells attached, and headdresses of animal horns or fur.

Cow dung is dried in the sun and burned as fuel.

Many Jurchen people are nomadic herders and live in large, circular tents.

Outer wall

Inner wall

Dung pile

Jurchen tents

Shepherd

Corner turret

Border castle

"Horse face" battle platform

Scaffolding

Moat

Winch for hauling up water

Water barrel

Measuring tools

15

Shaped like the long face of a horse, these battle platforms are used to shoot attackers who breach the other defenses.

The workers dig deep trenches to stop the Mongol cavalry's horses.

The earth dug to make the trench is piled up to build the wall.

The grain stores will be a target for thieves if the harvest fails, so they are closely guarded.

Families farm plots of land along the Great Wall.

A newborn has her first glimpse of the outside world.

Yan Mountains

Watchtower

Main wall

Watchtower

Local government offices

Granaries

Wheat field

Civilian quarters

Cowshed

Merchant's tent

Water cart

Ox cart

Cattle trader

Cavalry patrol

16

Can you find a bull scratching his back?

THE MING GREAT WALL
JUYONG PASS, 1571 CE

Haunted by a century under Mongol control, China's Ming rulers have rebuilt and strengthened the Great Wall, and it is now more invincible than ever. Just a few hours' gallop from Beijing, the fortress at the Juyong mountain pass has suffered Mongol attacks in the past, but these days life is peaceful. In the golden sunshine of a fall afternoon, a steady stream of travelers make their way through the arch beneath the pass's old stone Cloud Platform, while out in the fields, farm workers bring in the harvest to prepare for winter.

Buddhist temple

Library

Marble railings

Farming tools shop

Teahouse

Leather shop

Cloud Platform

Drying fruit

Drying vegetables

Tannery

Dried maize

Dried meat

Dried chilies

Water well

Maize store

17

The largest watchtower on the Great Wall, the Nine-Eyed Tower has nine windows on each side.

Can you spot a little piglet that has lost her way?

Nine-Eyed Tower

Jiankou Great Wall

Gate tower

Horse barrier

Arrow tower

Barracks

Silk shop

Guesthouse

Saddle shop

Restaurant

Guards

Camel train

Pigsty

Sheep pen

Farmer

Horse trader

Spy

18

 A spy in the emperor's secret police is questioning travelers coming through the gate.

 The strong horses bred in the north have a high value at market.

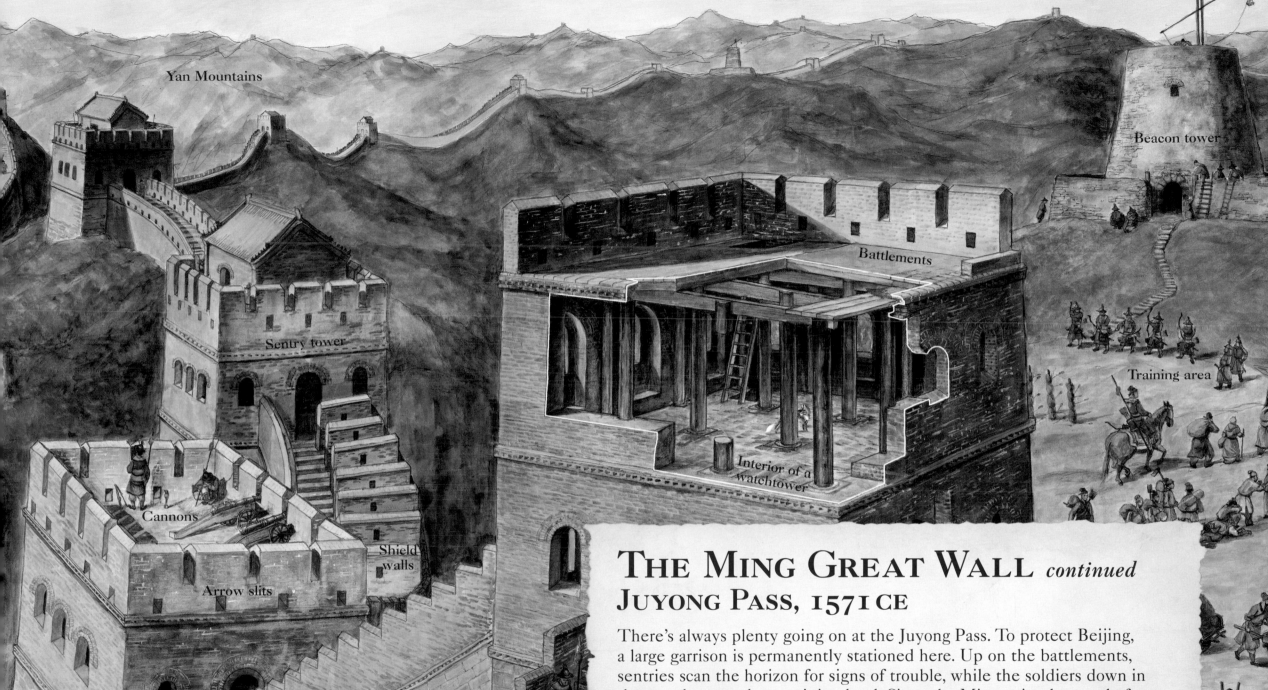

An off-duty sentry is snoozing in the afternoon sunshine.

The large brick watchtowers have space for soldiers to sleep and store their weapons and provisions.

Yan Mountains

Beacon tower

Battlements

Sentry tower

Training area

Cannons

Interior of a watchtower

Shield walls

Arrow slits

THE MING GREAT WALL *continued*
JUYONG PASS, 1571 CE

There's always plenty going on at the Juyong Pass. To protect Beijing, a large garrison is permanently stationed here. Up on the battlements, sentries scan the horizon for signs of trouble, while the soldiers down in the parade ground are training hard. Since the Ming gained control of territory north of the wall, Juyong Pass has been an important trading hub. Merchants and traders pass through all day long, but they must stop at the main gate tower to have their goods inspected and taxed. For some travelers, the pass makes an ideal place to pause for a bite to eat or a bed for the night.

19

Shield walls give defenders extra protection from attackers who have climbed onto the wall.

Below the beacon tower, soldiers are practicing their archery skills.

An overseer pleads with Qi Jiguang to allow more time to finish his work.

 The bricks are baked slowly at a high temperature in underground kilns.

THE MING GREAT WALL *continued*
GUBEIKOU, 1571 CE

When Mongol raiders last swooped down to attack Beijing, they broke through the weakly defended pass at Gubeikou. The border wall northeast of the city must be reinforced, and the emperor has called on his brilliant military general Qi Jiguang—fresh from defending the coast from pirate attacks—to mastermind the work. Qi sets his workers to build huge watchtowers made of strong bricks all along the wall's length. The new towers will house dozens of battle-ready soldiers, securing the Great Wall against the northern nomads once again.

Yan Mountains

Gubeikou Great Wall

Barracks

Military training

Baked bricks

Qi Jiguang

Brick kilns

Brick-drying sheds

Supervising soldiers

Coal

Firewood

Riddle (sifting tool)

Kiln entrance

Winch

Brick carriers

Unbaked bricks

Mules carrying bricks

20

 Mud is packed into a wooden mold to shape the bricks.

 Can you spot this worker? He is pouring water over the bricks to cool them and make them stronge

 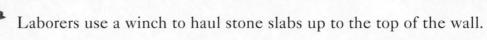
Simatai Great Wall

With sheer drops on either side, the dangerous path along the Simatai Great Wall is not for the faint-hearted.

Sentry

Sentry post

Arrow slits

Outer battlements

Inner parapet wall

Winch

Quarry

Bricklayer

Enemy spies

21

 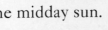

A silk merchant from Suzhou shows off the quality of his fabrics to a group of merchants from western China.

Red Rock
Canyon

Zhenbeitai Tower

Horse pen

Grain stores

Mongol cart train

Monks

Grain seller

Mongol tent
(*ger*)

Guard

Blacksmith

Government inspector

Pancake stall

Horses
for sale

Mongol
travelers

 An interested buyer inspects a horse's teeth to check its age and health. Can you spot an old man collecting manure to sell as fuel?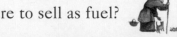

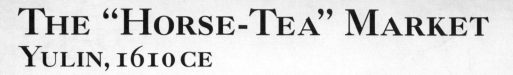

THE "HORSE-TEA" MARKET
YULIN, 1610 CE

The Great Wall is now strong and secure but the Ming realize that peace with the Mongols will never last without diplomacy and trade. They set up "horse-tea" markets along the border, nicknamed after the most popular goods exchanged. The biggest is staged midway along the wall, watched over by the guards of the massive Zhenbeitai Tower. Twice a year, merchants flock here from all over China to exchange tea, medicines, alcohol, and silks with Mongol traders, whose fine horses, animal hides, and leather goods are sought after back home.

Gate tower

Sheep for sale

Corner turret

Kuangong City

Sentry tower

Yima City

Brick battlements

Guards

Wall made of rammed earth

Camel saddles

23

After being unloaded, the camels are taking a well-earned rest.

A vet is treating a sick cow.

Jiumenkou means "Nine Gates Pass," after the number of arches in the bridge.

Soldiers hidden in the secret tunnel will jump out to attack invader

Watchtower

Tunnel entrance

Fortress

Artillery

Ming flag

Arrow slits

Hoisting up weapons

DEFENDING THE BRIDGE
JIUMENKOU PASS, 1644 CE

These are uneasy moments for the soldiers guarding the fortified bridge at the Jiumenkou Pass. An army of peasant rebels has stormed Beijing, and the emperor is dead. Tang Tong, once a trusted general, has defected to the rebels, and is advancing toward the bridge at the head of a massive army. As the distant war cries grow louder, the bridge defenders reach for their weapons and prepare to fight. Tang Tong's advance will end in failure but it won't be long before the Ming are under attack once more.

Fishing net

Fishing boat

Rebels disguised as fishermen are planning to set fire to the bridge's wooden gates.

The gates allow water to flow through while blocking enemy acce

Tang Tong has marched an army of 20,000 rebels across the mountains.

Can you find these defending soldiers fleeing to safety on the bridge?

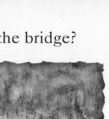

The Ming generals meet to plan how to respond. They are confident the bridge defenses can be held.

Yan Mountains

Rebel army

Patrol boat

Jiujiang River

Weapons stores

Barracks

Fortress

Fire for lighting cannons

Artillery

Sulfur

Charcoal

Messenger

Saltpeter

Three-barreled guns

Military commanders

Horse ramp

Water gate

Fortress

Cannon

25

Charcoal, sulfur, and a chemical called saltpeter are mixed to make gunpowder.

A soldier wields his three-barreled shotgun, a deadly weapon.

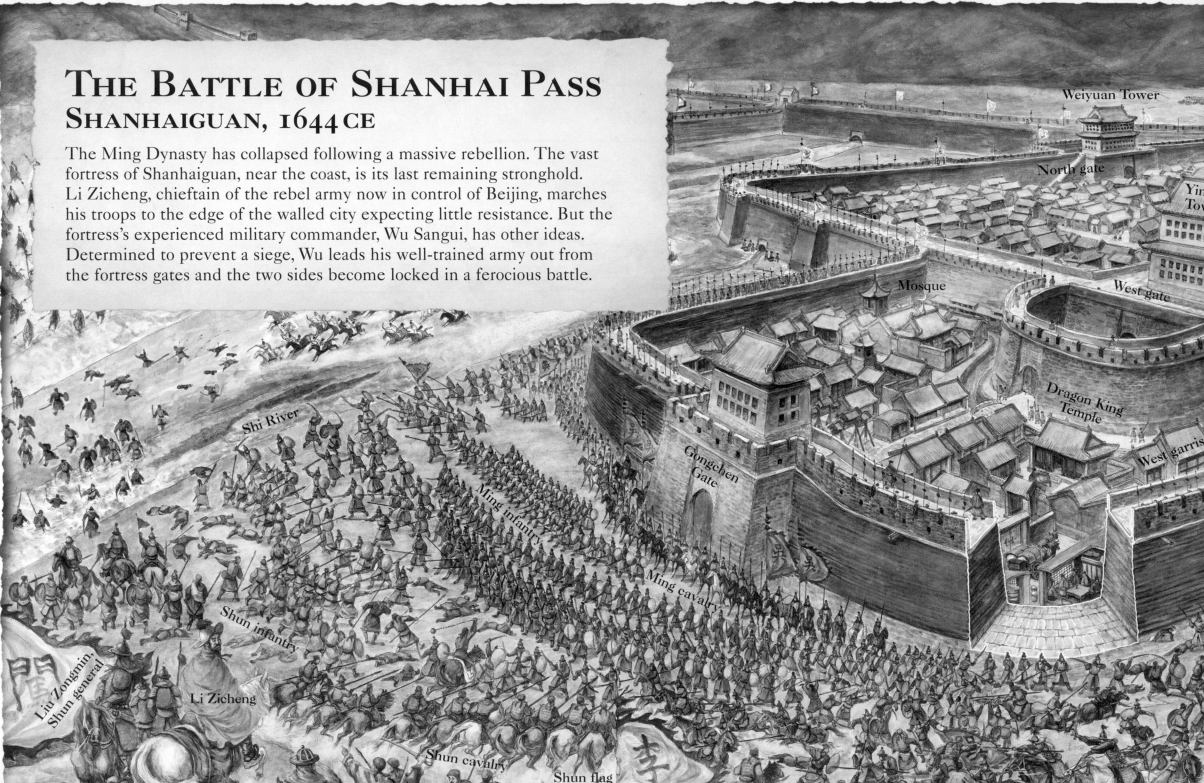

THE BATTLE OF SHANHAI PASS
SHANHAIGUAN, 1644 CE

The Ming Dynasty has collapsed following a massive rebellion. The vast fortress of Shanhaiguan, near the coast, is its last remaining stronghold. Li Zicheng, chieftain of the rebel army now in control of Beijing, marches his troops to the edge of the walled city expecting little resistance. But the fortress's experienced military commander, Wu Sangui, has other ideas. Determined to prevent a siege, Wu leads his well-trained army out from the fortress gates and the two sides become locked in a ferocious battle.

Weiyuan Tower

North gate

Yin Tov

Mosque

West gate

Dragon King Temple

West garrise

Shi River

Ming infantry

Gongchen Gate

Ming cavalry

Shun infantry

Liu Zongmin, Shun general

Li Zicheng

Shun cavalry

Shun flag

Zhu Silang, the emperor's son

Wu Xiang, Wu Sangui's father

Niu Jinxing, Li's deputy

Wu Sangui

Li has angered Wu by taking his father, as well as the former emperor's son, hostage.   The Ming soldiers' families shelter from the fighting inside the fortress wa

Zhendong
Tower

Yan Mountains

Fuyuan Tower

Northeast
turret

Drum and Bell
Tower

East garrison

Wangyang
Tower

East gate

Confucius school

Courier station

Main street

South gate

City guards

Sluice gate

Shun
infantry

27

The battle-hardened guards of the fortress keep watch for intruders.

Cannons are the Ming's most effective weapon. Can you see this one being fired?

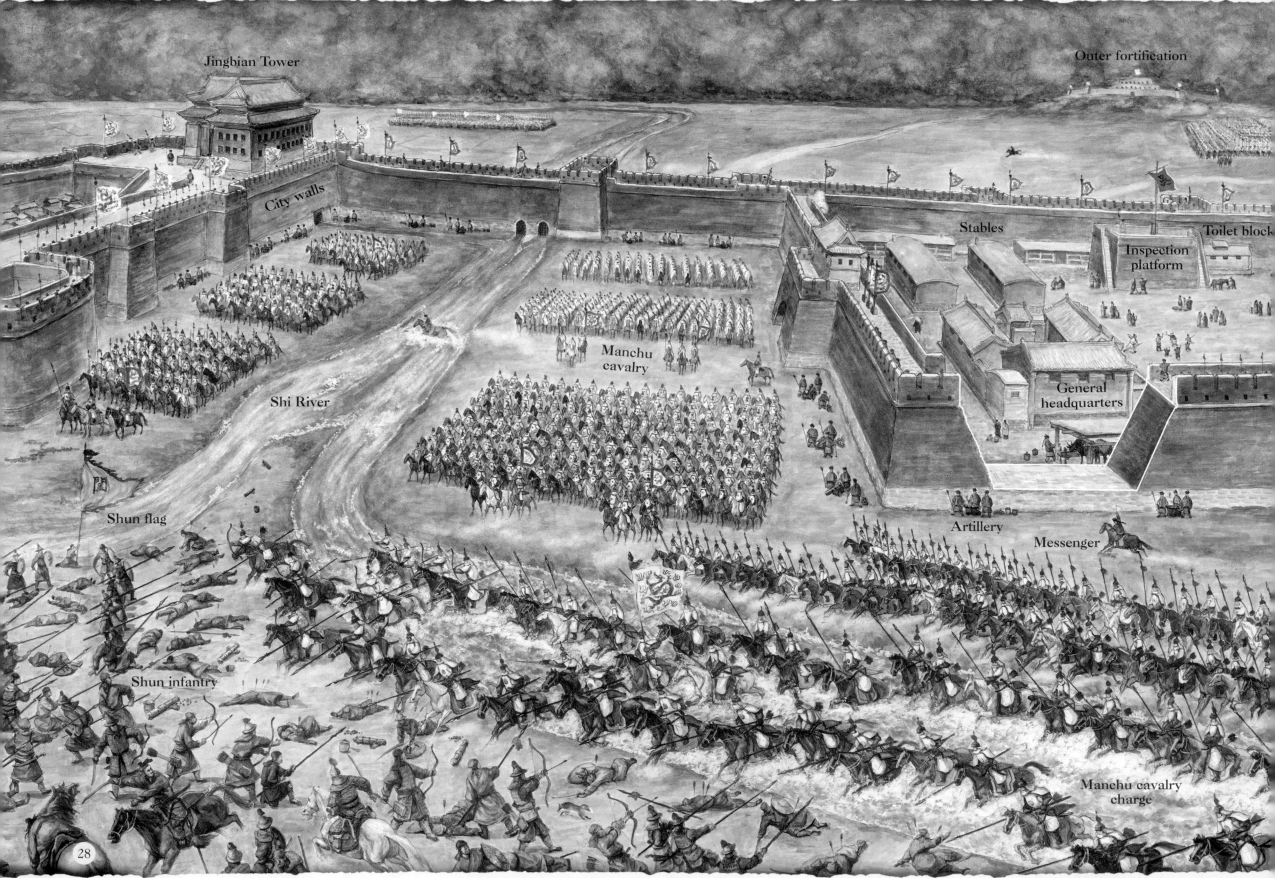

Jingbian Tower

Outer fortification

City walls

Stables

Toilet block

Inspection platform

Manchu cavalry

General headquarters

Shi River

Artillery

Messenger

Shun flag

Shun infantry

Manchu cavalry charge

 The rebels begin to retreat when they see the Manchu cavalry advancing. The Manchu warriors attack Li's troops using long lances.

The Nanyi Great Wall connects the walled city with Old Dragon's Head.

The Manchu officers hold their cavalry units back, waiting for the rebels to tire.

Approaching sandstorm

tchens

Nanyi Great Wall

Dormitories

Wing City
(local military headquarters)

Messenger

Manchu
cavalry

Prince
Dodo

Prince
Ajige

THE BATTLE OF SHANHAI PASS *continued*
SHANHAIGUAN, 1644 CE

There is an even bigger threat to the Ming. To the northeast lie the lands of the Manchu people, descendants of the Jurchens, who have united and are poised to invade. Realizing that the days of the Ming are numbered, General Wu has made a secret alliance with the Manchu leader, Dorgon. He promises to hand over power if they help defeat the rebels. Wu opens the city gates to the Manchu army and they enter the battlefield. When a sudden wind whips up a sandstorm the Manchu cavalry, led by Dorgon's brothers, take advantage of the confusion. They charge Li's men and force them to flee back to Beijing.

Dorgon's brother, Prince Ajige, leads the Manchu cavalry charge. He is brave but not very clever.

Prince Dodo, another brother, is a ruthless commander.

Dorgon will rule China as regent for the new Qing emperor, his nephew, who is just five years old.

Manchu men braid their hair in a long ponytail called a *queu*

Chenghai Tower

Yan Mountains

Barracks

Military offices

Dorgon

Manchu cavalry

Old Dragon's Head Fortress

Hot oil

Wooden logs

Stone balls

Manchu cavalry

Can you spot a Manchu horseman riding up a ramp inside the fortress?

The weaponry on show includes missiles that can be hurled at enemies below.

The fortress bears the flags of the Plain White Banner; this is one of the Manchu army's eight banners (divisions), each of which is named after its flag color.

Battle platform

Bohai Gulf

THE BATTLE OF SHANHAI PASS *continued*
SHANHAIGUAN, 1644 CE

At the Old Dragon's Head fortress, the Great Wall meets the sea. After the triumph over the peasant rebels, General Wu's soldiers join the Manchu army and Dorgon arrives at the sea fortress to inspect his victorious troops from the ramparts. From here they will go on to force Li Zicheng out of Beijing and establish a new dynasty—the Qing. It is the end for the Great Wall as a military barrier. Now the land on both sides of the wall belongs to the Manchu, and its defenses are abandoned.

Cannon

Battle platform

Flag of the Plain White Banner

The sea fortress gets its name because it appears like a giant dragon's head jutting out into the ocean.

The Manchu cavalrymen wear feathers in their helmets and metal medallions on their tunics. Large boulders protect the fortress from the crashing waves.

A woman bellows at the workmen to stop making so much noise. They were supposed to finish a week ago.

Qilian Mountains

Rouyuan
Gate Tower

Corner turret

Gate
tower

Scaffolding

Banqueting
hall

Painter

Duty guards'
room

Western explo

Battlements

Workmen

Barbican

Ramme
earth w

A traveler takes a photo with his new camera, causing a local who is suspicious of this unfamiliar machine to run away in fear.

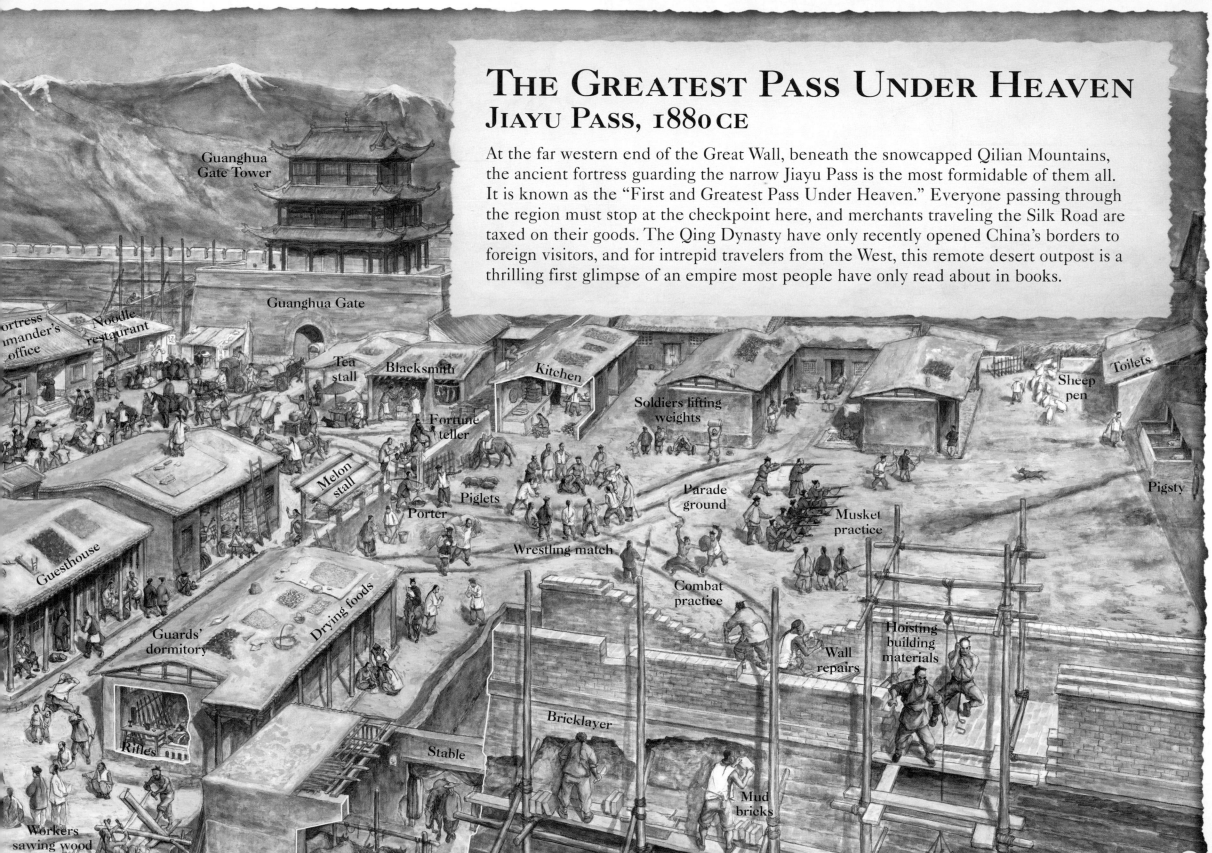

THE GREATEST PASS UNDER HEAVEN
JIAYU PASS, 1880 CE

At the far western end of the Great Wall, beneath the snowcapped Qilian Mountains, the ancient fortress guarding the narrow Jiayu Pass is the most formidable of them all. It is known as the "First and Greatest Pass Under Heaven." Everyone passing through the region must stop at the checkpoint here, and merchants traveling the Silk Road are taxed on their goods. The Qing Dynasty have only recently opened China's borders to foreign visitors, and for intrepid travelers from the West, this remote desert outpost is a thrilling first glimpse of an empire most people have only read about in books.

Guanghua Gate Tower

Guanghua Gate

Fortress commander's office

Noodle restaurant

Tea stall

Blacksmith

Kitchen

Soldiers lifting weights

Toilets

Sheep pen

Fortune teller

Melon stall

Piglets

Porter

Wrestling match

Parade ground

Musket practice

Pigsty

Combat practice

Guesthouse

Drying foods

Guards' dormitory

Wall repairs

Hoisting building materials

Rifles

Bricklayer

Stable

Mud bricks

Workers sawing wood

A convict is led through the gate on the way to prison.

This long-barreled rifle needs two people to operate it.

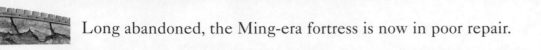

A wealthy young man discusses motoring with the prince.

Can you spot a dog barking at the noisy engine?

Battlements

Sentry post

Tumu Fortress wall

Ox-drawn wagon

Camel train

Prince Scipione Borghese

Interpreter

Camel-drawn wagon

Itala car (Italy)

Young official

Charles Godard

Auguste Pons

Paper toys

Contal cyclecar (France)

Workers

34

Camels have brought fuel from Beijing.

In second place is the Dutch car driven by a charming but penniless con artist who will later be arrested!

THE BEIJING TO PARIS RALLY
HUAILAI, 1907 CE

The crumbling walls of the old Tumu Fortress have witnessed some spectacles in their time, but nothing as extraordinary as this. Five noisy motor cars have sputtered into town, each driven by an eccentric European. The cars are racing from Beijing to far-off Paris in France—an almost impossible journey, with few roads and countless obstacles. No one has ever attempted anything like it before. As the drivers prepare to resume their journey, the locals gather in wonder at these strange new machines.

Fortress gate

Water spout

Corner turret

Spyker car (Netherlands)

De-Dion Bouton car (France)

Georges Cormier

De-Dion Bouton car (France)

Local official

Journalist

Victor Collignon

"Beijing to Paris"

Soldier

Sedan chair

Traveling barber

A journalist accompanies one of the French drivers. He's sending updates on the race to his newspaper in Paris.

A little boy sitting on his father's shoulders points at the car's steering wheel.

A senior official watches the commotion from the comfort of his sedan chair.

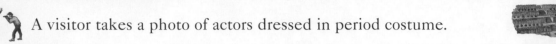

A visitor takes a photo of actors dressed in period costume.

The words of famous writers who have passed through are etched onto stone tablets.

Watchtower

Yan Lou
(Wild Goose Tower)

Museum

Stone inscriptions

Tianxian Gate

Tour group

Main courtyard gate

Offices

Hall

Pillar for
tethering
horses

The Yan Lou watchtower has been made into a museum.

Can you spot a young art student sketching a soldier?

This visitor has never mounted a horse before. It's harder than it looks!

A young boy is racing his friend the length of the battlements.

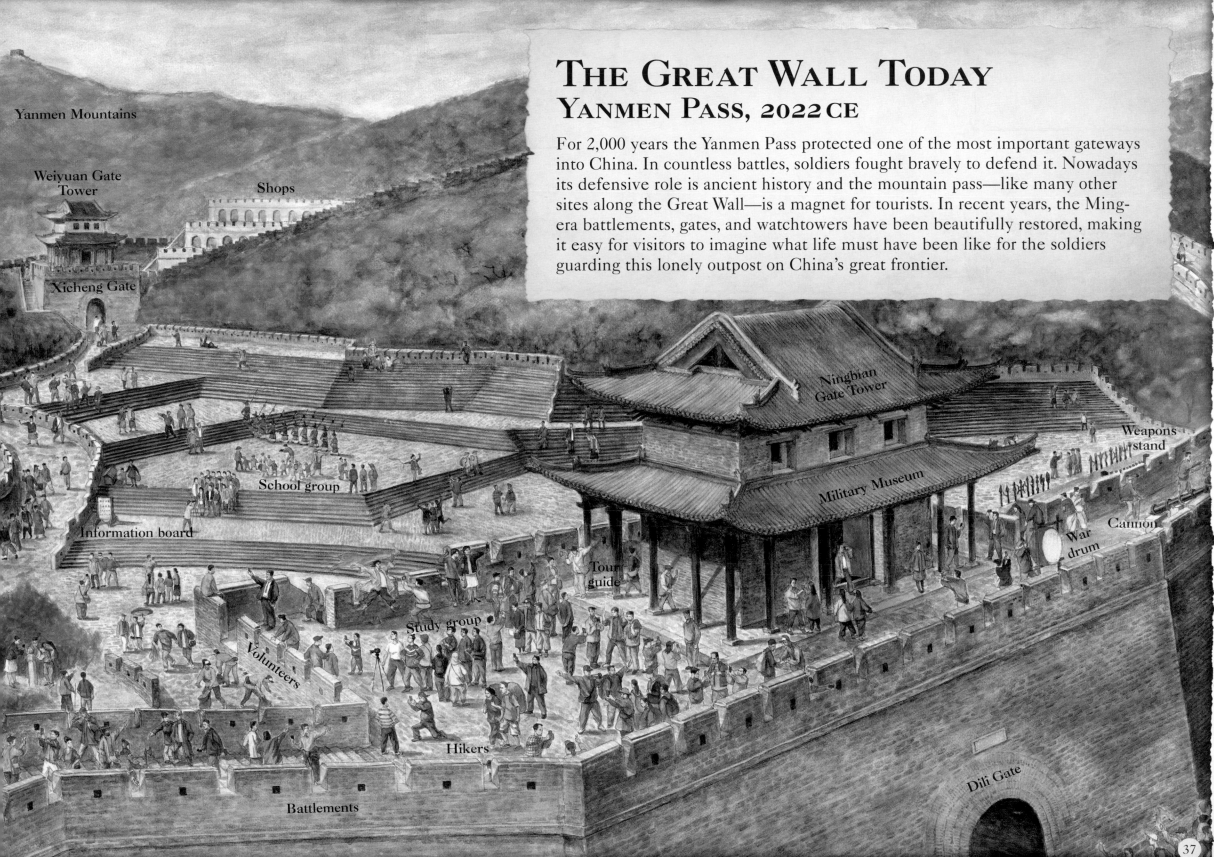

Volunteers lend a hand picking up litter dropped by tourists.

Yanmen Pass, or "Wild Goose Gate," is named after the geese who visit the area.

Yanmen Mountains

Weiyuan Gate Tower

Shops

Xicheng Gate

THE GREAT WALL TODAY
YANMEN PASS, 2022 CE

For 2,000 years the Yanmen Pass protected one of the most important gateways into China. In countless battles, soldiers fought bravely to defend it. Nowadays its defensive role is ancient history and the mountain pass—like many other sites along the Great Wall—is a magnet for tourists. In recent years, the Ming-era battlements, gates, and watchtowers have been beautifully restored, making it easy for visitors to imagine what life must have been like for the soldiers guarding this lonely outpost on China's great frontier.

Ningbian Gate Tower

Weapons stand

School group

Military Museum

Information board

Cannon

Tour guide

War drum

Study group

Volunteers

Hikers

Dili Gate

Battlements

37

Two backpackers have been hiking along the wall for a week—it's been an amazing trip!

The tour guide's entertaining stories bring the history of the tower alive.

THE GREAT WALL THROUGH THE AGES

Many dynasties contributed to the network of defensive barriers we call the Great Wall of China. The remains of all these individual structures now total 13,170 miles (21,196 km).

EASTERN ZHOU DYNASTY (770–256 BCE)

EARLY WALLS

Long before China became a large empire, the ancient Chinese built walls around their homes, farms, villages, and towns to keep out strangers and wild animals. Around 656 BCE, the kingdom of Chu—one of China's many small states—built a number of square forts along its border and connected them with ramparts. This was the first long wall.

WARRING STATES

By the 5th century BCE, larger kingdoms had swallowed up weaker ones, and by 300 BCE only seven rival states remained. The kingdoms of Qin, Zhao, and Yan built long walls to protect themselves from attacks by nomadic tribes in the north, as well as from each other. In 230 BCE, Ying Zheng, the ruthless king of the Qin, set about conquering each remaining kingdom one by one.

QIN DYNASTY (221–206 BCE)

CHINA UNIFIED

Ying Zheng defeated the last of the rival states in 221 BCE, uniting China for the first time. He declared himself emperor under the name Qin Shi Huang and brought in reforms, such a single currency, to bring his empire together.

NORTHERN ATTACKS

But China still faced a threat from its northern enemies. In 214 BCE, the emperor sent General Meng Tian to drive them out, and to keep them away he ordered the existing Zhao, Yan, and Qin walls to be linked together to form one long barrier.

THE ENDLESS WALL

It took nine years for one million workers to build new defenses to connect the walls. Many thousands died in terrible conditions. When it was finished, the Qin wall stretched for 1,850 miles (3,000 km). It became known as the "Endless Wall."

HAN DYNASTY (206 BCE–220 CE)

A PEACE DEAL

After Qin Shi Huang's death, an uprising led to a new dynasty seizing power—the Han. Meanwhile, the northern tribes united as the Xiongnu Empire, and continued their attacks. To secure lasting peace, many Han rulers were forced to offer a Han princess to each Xiongnu leader as a bride, and send gifts.

THE EMPIRE EXPANDS

In 141 BCE, a new emperor came to power, determined to end this humiliation. Emperor Wudi sent his generals on long expeditions to force out the Xiongnu. He expanded his empire to the north and west, and rebuilt and extended the Qin wall to protect it. When construction finished, the Han wall stretched for more than 4,500 miles (7,200 km).

THE SILK ROAD

The Han conquest of new lands made it possible to travel all the way from China to Europe, opening up the trading route known as the Silk Road. Chinese merchants grew rich selling luxury goods, and ideas spread along the route, too—Buddhism was introduced from India. To protect trade, new fortifications were built at key points along the wall.

THREE KINGDOMS TO THE TANG (220–907 CE)

PERIOD OF DISUNION

After the fall of the Han Dynasty, three different warlords claimed power. For several centuries China descended into civil war—an era known as the Period of Disunion. Existing walls deteriorated until the Northern Dynasties period (420–581 CE), when several rival kingdoms built new sections to protect themselves from invasion.

SUI DYNASTY

The fighting came to an end when the Sui Dynasty (581–618 CE) took power, reuniting China once again. The ruthless Emperor Yang forced a million laborers to renovate the wall. Again, many didn't survive.

TANG DYNASTY

The Sui Dynasty was short-lived, but under the long rule of the powerful Tang Dynasty (618–907 CE), Chinese culture blossomed. The Tang built alliances with the northern nomads, bringing peace. Trade along the Silk Road reached its peak, and brought prosperity. During this Golden Age, the Great Wall lay mostly abandoned.

THE LIAO TO THE YUAN DYNASTIES (916–1368 CE)

SONG RULE

The Tang fell, and in the northeast borderlands a nomad group called the Qidans united to establish the Liao Dynasty in 916 CE. The Han Chinese people now had less territo[r] but continued to rule in the south under the Song Dynasty (960–1279 CE) Most of the Great Wall now lay far to the north, outside their lands.

JIN DYNASTY

In 1115 CE, another northeastern group called the Jurchens toppled the Liao and founded the Jin Dynasty. Work soon began on a new wall, made of earth, with a trench dug alongside. The Jin fought wars against the Song, gaining territory, but their power was not to last.

MONGOL CONQUEST

To the north of the Jin Empire, the nomadic tribes that had for so long launched raids on China were brilliantly united under Genghis Khan. In 1207 CE, his Mongol caval[ry] first attacked the lands south of the border. By 1279 CE, the Mongol conquest was complete. All of Chin[a] now lay in the hands of the Mongol[s] who ruled as the Yuan Dynasty.

ING DYNASTY (368–1644)

CHINESE RULE RESTORED

ter four centuries of nomadic
le in the north, the Han Chinese
ople finally reestablished control
China. Determined to prevent
rther invasion, the Ming began
e most ambitious Great Wall
nstruction project ever seen, which
ntinued throughout their rule.

HE MING GREAT WALL

he techniques and materials the
ing used were far more advanced
an anything ever seen before. To
tter protect the capital, Beijing,
ey built a strong new wall of stone
d brick, and reinforced it with
w battlements, large watchtowers,
d military fortresses. In places, the
ll reached up to 25 ft (8 m) high,
d was wide enough for five horses
ride side by side. At 5,500 miles
850 km), the Ming wall was the
ngest ever built, and many of its
mains are still preserved today.

OWNFALL OF THE MING

pay for the wall, the Ming raised
ge taxes, and in time—facing
rdship and famine—the people
belled. As the Ming Dynasty fell
art, another powerful group from
e northeast—the Manchus—took
vantage of the chaos. In 1644,
Ming general allowed the Manchu
valry to enter China through a
te in the wall, and the Manchus
ickly overthrew the Ming.

QING DYNASTY TO TODAY (1644–present)

THE WALL ABANDONED

The Qing Dynasty, set up by the
Manchus, now ruled over a much
larger empire, and the border
shifted far to the north of the Great
Wall. Confident in their power,
the new rulers didn't see much
point in renovating the wall.
Its defenses were abandoned
and it fell into disrepair.

THE MODERN ERA

In the 1950s, the Chinese
government started to preserve
and restore the Great Wall, and
began opening it up to tourism.
In 1987, it was made a UNESCO
World Heritage Site, and now
millions of tourists visit various
parts of it every year. Yet the wall is
under threat. Over the centuries,
many people have taken its bricks
for their own buildings, and natural
forces have also taken their toll.
The government has passed laws
to prevent people damaging the
wall, and is now using modern
technology to help conserve it, so
that this ancient wonder can be
enjoyed by future generations.

TIME-TRAVELING QUIZ

Search through the pages of the
book to see what Hong Yu, our
cunning, time-traveling fox,
is getting up to.

PAGES 4–5

Hong Yu has concealed
herself in the grass. What
is she hiding from?

PAGES 6–7

Our red fox has found a
place by the wall to rest.
Can you spot her?

PAGES 8–9

Hong Yu is excited by the
snow. What might she be
looking for buried below?

PAGES 10–11

What will Hong Yu find
when she reaches the
top of the ladder?

PAGES 12–13

Time-traveling is thirsty
work in this heat! Where's
Hong Yu having a drink?

PAGES 14–15

Our greedy fox has
followed her nose to the
kitchen. Can you find her?

PAGES 16–17

She's snoozing in the sun
close to a food vendor.
What has she just eaten?

PAGES 18–19

The clever fox has been
climbing ladders again.
Where is she now?

PAGES 20–21

Hong Yu's on a secret
mission. Who is she
spying on?

PAGES 22–23

Delicious food is never far
away at a market. What's
on the menu today?

PAGES 24–25

Hong Yu has found a place
to hide. But how is she
going to get out?

PAGES 26–27

Hong Yu needs to find her
way back into the fortress.
How will she get in?

PAGES 28–29

Hong Yu's caught up in
the fighting and needs
help! Can you see her?

PAGES 30–31

Our fox is safe but wants
to avoid the soldiers.
Where's she gone now?

PAGES 32–33

A fox needs some shade
on a hot day. But which
pillar is she behind?

PAGES 34–35

Hong Yu is off on her
travels again. Which team
is she helping?

PAGES 36–37

Our favorite fox has made
it to the present day.
Where's she off to next?

Glossary

Alliance An agreement between people or countries to work together to achieve a shared goal.

Arrow slit An small opening in a building through which an archer can shoot arrows.

Artillery The part of an army that uses large weapons such as cannons.

Barbican A defensive tower at the entrance to a fortress.

Barracks The building or group of buildings where soldiers live.

Battle platform A raised structure along the Great Wall from which defenders could keep a lookout for the enemy or launch an attack.

Battlements A wall around the top of a fortification with openings for defenders to shoot through.

BCE Before Common Era (see CE).

Beacon tower A tower used to send information by smoke or fire signals.

Buddhist A person who follows the teachings of Buddhism, one of the world's major religions.

Caravan A group of people traveling together for safety, often using pack animals such as camels.

Cavalry The part of an army that fights on horseback.

CE Common Era. The years from 1 CE to the present day.

Convict A person who is serving a prison sentence.

Courtier The advisors and favorites of a king or queen.

Dynasty A series or rulers from the same family, who pass power down from generation to generation.

Frontier The border between two countries.

Garrison A group of soldiers stationed in a fortress or town to defend it.

Gate tower A building above a gate used as a watchtower or as a base to defend against attack.

Han people The ethnic group that makes up the majority of the Chinese population. Starting with the Han Dynasty, Han people ruled China for long periods of its history.

Infantry The part of an army that fights on foot.

Inscription Writing that is carved into something such as a stone tablet.

Jurchen people An ethnic group who lived in northeastern China and ruled the country as the Jin Dynasty from 1115 to 1234 CE.

Kiln A large, very hot oven used to bake and dry bricks or clay.

Lady-in-waiting A female attendant to a queen or princess at court.

Lime A white substance used to make the mortar (paste) that binds bricks together.

Manchu people An ethnic group descended from the Jurchen people who ruled China from 1644 to 1912 CE as the Qing Dynasty.

Mongol people An ethnic group from northern China and modern-day Mongolia. Historically, the Mongols were nomadic tribespeople. They united as the Mongol Empire and ruled China as the Yuan Dynasty from 1271 to 1368 CE.

Nomad A person who moves from place to place rather than living in one location. Nomads are usually animal herders.

Parapet A low wall around the top of a fortification.

Pass A narrow route between mountains. Mountain passes were heavily guarded along the Great Wall, with checkpoints to control the entry and exit of people and goods.

Peasant A poor person with few rights who works on the land.

Rammed earth A building method in which wet earth and other materials are rammed hard into the ground with a special tool. This method was used to build many sections of the Great Wall.

Ramparts The earth walls of a fortification, usually with stone walls on top of them.

Regent A person who governs a country in place of the official ruler, usually because the official ruler is too young or ill to rule themselves.

Sedan chair An enclosed chair that is mounted on poles and carried by two people.

Sentry A soldier who guards the entry to a building or other place.

Shaman A priest or healer believed to have a special connection with the spirit world.

Shrine A sacred place devoted to a specific holy person, god, or object.

Shuttlecock A small object made from overlapping feathers fixed to a cork or rubber base.

Siege A military operation in which soldiers surround a place in order to force the people inside it to surrender.

Silk Road An important overland trade route through Central Asia, named after China's most valuable export.

Sluice gate A barrier across a water current that controls its flow.

Stronghold A fortress, or a place with strong defenses.

Tannery A place where animal skins are treated with chemicals to make them into leather.

Trench A long channel dug in the ground by soldiers to protect themselves from the enemy.

Tunic An item of clothing worn on the top part of the body.

Turret A small tower built at the corner of a fortification.

Winch A device used to lift heavy objects by winding a rope around a drum.

Xiongnu Nomadic people from northern China, who united under Modun Shanyu and formed an empire in the late 3rd century BCE.

The Illustrator

DU FEI was born in Beijing, and has almost 30 years' experience as a professor of mural painting and artistic creation. He specializes in painting realistic works portraying Chinese history and traditional culture. His work encompasses a variety of art forms, from murals and oil painting to sculpture and ceramics, and has been displayed in public spaces including museums, stadiums, parks, and subways. His best-known works include *The Development of Textile and Clothing in Ancient China* and *The Great Cathay*. He also illustrated DK's *China Through Time*.

The Consultant

William Lindsay OBE made a journey of 1,535 miles (2,470 km) on foot along the Great Wall in 1987. He settled in China in 1990 to explore, research, and contribute to the conservation of the monument. He has since written seven books, curated ten exhibitions, and presented the Great Wall story through a number of internationally broadcast documentaries.